ESSENTIAL **DK** COMPUTERS

MULTIMEDIA

CREATING
PRESENTATIONS

ABOUT THIS BOOK

Creating Presentations is an easy-to-follow introduction to Microsoft's PowerPoint® 2000 program. This book is for anyone who has no, or very little, experience of using PowerPoint.

POWERPOINT 2000 IS A HIGHLY sophisticated piece of software. *Creating Presentations* introduces the essential features of the program, from converting predefined presentations to your own needs, to designing complete presentations from scratch, adding and modifying text, images, sounds, animations, and charts.

The chapters and the subsections use a step-by-step approach. Virtually every step is accompanied by an illustration showing how your screen should look at each stage. The screen images are either full-screen or focus on an important detail that you'll see on your own screen. If you work through the steps, you'll soon start feeling comfortable that you're learning and making progress.

The book contains several features to help you understand both what is happening on-screen and what you need to do. A labeled PowerPoint window is included to show you

where to find the important elements that are used in PowerPoint. This is followed by an illustration of the rows of buttons, or "toolbars," at the top of the screen, to help you find your way around these invaluable, but initially perplexing, controls.

Command keys, such as ENTER and CTRL, are shown in rectangles (e.g. [Enter↵] and [Ctrl]) so that there's no confusion over whether, for example, you should press the [Ctrl] key, or type the letters "ctrl". Cross-references are shown in the text as left- or right-hand page icons: ◁ and ▷. The page number and the reference are shown at the foot of the page.

In addition to the step-by-step sections of the book, there are also boxes that describe and explain particular PowerPoint features in detail, and tip boxes that provide alternative methods and shortcuts. Finally, at the back of the book, you will find a glossary explaining new terms and a comprehensive index.

ESSENTIAL **DK** COMPUTERS

MULTIMEDIA

CREATING PRESENTATIONS

TERRY BURROWS

A Dorling Kindersley Book

Dorling Kindersley
LONDON, NEW YORK, DELHI, SYDNEY
PARIS, MUNICH, JOHANNESBURG

Produced for Dorling Kindersley Limited by
Design Revolution, Queens Park Villa,
30 West Drive, Brighton, East Sussex BN2 2GE

EDITORIAL DIRECTOR Ian Whitelaw
SENIOR DESIGNER Andy Ashdown
PROJECT EDITOR John Watson
DESIGNER Paul Bowler

MANAGING EDITOR Sharon Lucas
SENIOR MANAGING ART EDITOR Derek Coombes
DTP DESIGNER Sonia Charbonnier
PRODUCTION CONTROLLER Wendy Penn

Published in Great Britain in 2000 by
Dorling Kindersley Limited,
9 Henrietta Street, London WC2E 8PS

2 4 6 8 10 9 7 5 3 1

Color reproduced by First Impressions, London
Printed in Italy by Graphicom

For our complete
catalog visit
www.dk.com

CONTENTS

STARTING POWERPOINT

Although PowerPoint 2000 is recognizable from its appearance as a part of the Office 2000 suite of programs, it uniquely blends multimedia features into a powerful presentation tool.

WHAT IS POWERPOINT 2000?

At some point, most of us have to give a presentation. This could mean telling a group of friends how to get from one location to another, or it could be a president of a corporation talking to the shareholders. However, in both situations the basic aim is to convey information.

Although it is possible to stand and read from a script, it's far easier to retain interest and consolidate the message by using visual cues. For an effective presentation, the speaker must back up the script with overhead projections, slides, handouts, and speaker's notes.

WHAT IS A POWERPOINT PRESENTATION?

Imagine a computer program that can structure and create dynamic visual presentations, which include full-color images, sounds, animations, charts, and graphs. Imagine, too, that it enables you to prepare handouts to accompany each slide in your presentation. Finally, imagine that you could run the presentation on your computer. Microsoft PowerPoint 2000 is capable of all this and more.

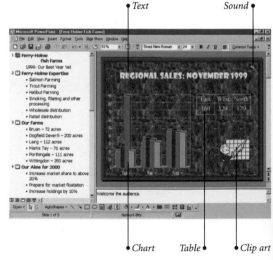

Text *Sound*

Chart *Table* *Clip art*

LAUNCHING POWERPOINT

To run PowerPoint 2000, switch on your PC and go into Windows – in most cases this should happen automatically.

Microsoft PowerPoint 2000 will work happily with Windows 95, Windows 98, and Windows NT.

THE POWERPOINT DIALOG BOX
● Click on the **Start** button on the Task bar.
● From the pop-up menu, point to **Program**.
● From the drop-down menu, click on **Microsoft PowerPoint**.
● If you can't find PowerPoint in the **Program** folder, then it probably means that the software has not been installed. PowerPoint 2000 is generally acquired as a part of the Microsoft Office 2000 suite of programs. If you have a problem, go back to the original CDs – or, better still, get someone more experienced to do it for you.
● Each time you launch PowerPoint 2000, the first screen that you come into contact with is a PowerPoint dialog box. This provides you with four options before you finally get to see the main **PowerPoint** window .

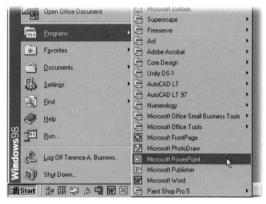

THE POWERPOINT WINDOW

The main body of the dialog box is split into two segments. On the left-hand side you are given an overview of the structure and content of the different slides that make up your presentation. The screen on the right shows the currently active slide. This is the screen in which you can edit and add to the contents of the slide.

THE STRUCTURE OF THE WINDOW

1 Slide icon
2 Title bar
3 Menu bar
4 Standard toolbar
5 Formatting toolbar
6 Outline pane
7 Slide pane
8 Slide template
9 Minimize
10 Maximize
11 Close
12 Views toolbar
13 Slide counter
14 Outline scrollbar
15 Drawing toolbar
16 Notes pane
17 Notes scrollbar

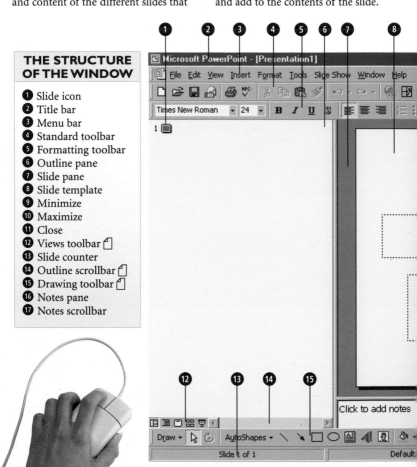

30 The Outline View

16 Displaying Your Presentation on Screen

MOVING THE TOOLBARS

If the Formatting toolbar does not appear below the Standard toolbar, place the cursor over the Formatting toolbar "handle." When the four-headed arrow appears (right), hold down the mouse button and drag the toolbar into position.

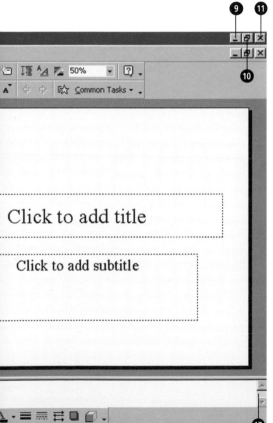

Click to add title

Click to add subtitle

Toolbar layout options

You are not limited to having the toolbars positioned along the top of the screen – it's possible to place them anywhere in the main dialog box. A commonly used alternative is to drag the toolbars to either side of the screen where they appear as vertical bars. You can either click on the toolbar handle or on an inactive part of the toolbar and drag it to your preferred location.

48 **The Drawing Toolbar**

THE POWERPOINT TOOLBARS

The icons below the Menu bar are grouped into toolbars. When PowerPoint 2000 is first installed, the two main toolbars – Standard and Formatting – occupy a single row; one is shown below

the other here for clarity. At the foot of the window when you first run PowerPoint 2000, the Drawing toolbar appears, which contains the common graphics commands that can be applied to your presentations.

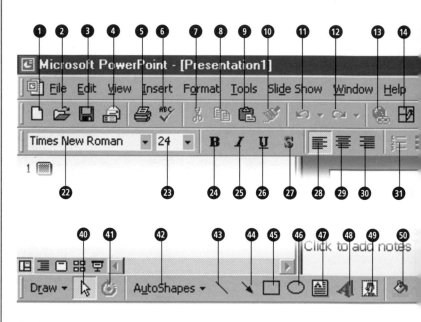

THE FORMATTING TOOLBAR		
22 Font	28 Align left	34 Decrease font size
23 Font size	29 Center	35 Promote
24 Bold	30 Align right	36 Demote
25 Italic	31 Numbered list	37 Animation effects
26 Underline	32 Bulleted list	38 Common task menu
27 Shadow	33 Increase font size	39 More buttons

40 **Changing the Font**

40 **Changing the Font Size**

THE STANDARD TOOLBAR

1. New
2. Open
3. Save
4. Email
5. Print
6. Spelling
7. Cut
8. Copy
9. Paste
10. Format painter
11. Undo
12. Redo
13. Insert hyperlink
14. Tables and borders
15. Insert table
16. Insert chart
17. New slide
18. Expand all
19. Show formatting
20. Grayscale preview
21. Zoom

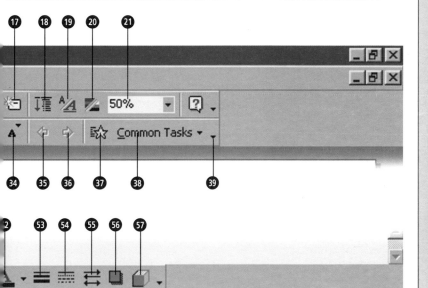

THE DRAWING TOOLBAR

40. Select objects
41. Free rotate
42. AutoShapes menu
43. Line
44. Arrow
45. Rectangle
46. Oval
47. Text box
48. Insert WordArt
49. Insert Clip Art
50. Fill color
51. Line color
52. Font color
53. Line style
54. Dash style
55. Arrow style
56. Shadow
57. 3-D

50 Using
WordArt

A FIRST PRESENTATION

Now that you've been introduced to the main dialog box used in PowerPoint 2000, it's time to begin to create your first presentation using PowerPoint 2000's AutoContent Wizard.

THE AUTOCONTENT WIZARD

If you've never given a presentation before, the AutoContent Wizard is the ideal place to begin. The basic unit that you work with in PowerPoint is a "slide," which is like a photographic slide, and you create a sequence of slides that becomes your presentation. By working through a series of AutoContent screens, answering questions and evaluating options, you can begin setting up the Title slide – the first slide – and create a basic outline of what you will produce ⌐. At this stage we're concentrating on the opening and the overall shape of the presentation.

STARTING THE WIZARD

● Start PowerPoint 2000. When the PowerPoint window appears, click on the **AutoContent Wizard** radio button and then click on **OK**.

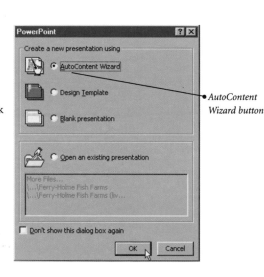

AutoContent Wizard button

Assistance
When you first use the AutoContent Wizard, the Office Assistant may intrude and ask if you want some help. Click on the **NO** button to send your assistant packing.

16 **Displaying Your Presentation On-Screen**

● The first screen of the AutoContent Wizard appears. This lists the stages to go through to create a presentation.

● Click on **Next>** to move to **Presentation Type**.

PRESENTATION TYPES

The first active screen of the AutoContent Wizard allows you to specify the type of presentation that most closely fits your requirements. The buttons in the center of the dialog box contain categories of presentation, such as **Corporate** or **Projects** or **General** (the button marked **All** contains all of the options covered by the other five buttons). The presentations available for each category are shown in the scrolling list on the right-hand side of the dialog box.

CATEGORY BUTTONS

● Click on one of the category buttons and then on one of the choices from the accompanying list.

● Click on **Next>** to move to AutoContent Wizard's second active screen.

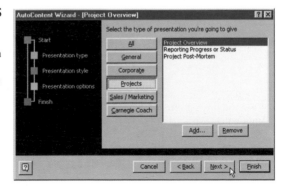

STYLES AND OTHER OPTIONS

The second of the AutoContent Wizard's active screens lets you specify the nature of the presentation and how it is eventually going to be viewed. There are five options, three of which are concerned with the type of media to be projected.

CHOOSING THE TYPE OF OUTPUT

ON-SCREEN
This creates dynamic presentations that can be executed by PowerPoint 2000 to run on a computer. You have the option of changing slides at the press of a key or programming them so that they change at specific time intervals. In this book, step-by-step instructions are given for creating this type of presentation alone, although there are other types of output.

WEB PRESENTATION
By using this option you can turn a presentation into a self-contained website on the World Wide Web.

OVERHEADS AND SLIDES
The remaining three options are for the preparation of presentations that are to be viewed using an overhead projector or 35mm slides.

1 MAKING YOUR SELECTION
● Select the type of presentation output you want to use by clicking on the button.
● Click on **Next**>.

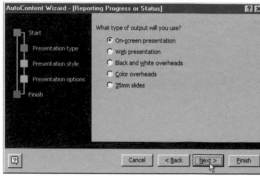

2 PRESENTATION OPTIONS

● The AutoContent Wizard's third active screen allows you to give your presentation a title and specify any footnotes that will appear on each slide.

● Enter the presentation's title in the first text box.

● If you want to add a footnote to be shown at the bottom of every slide, enter it in the second text box.

● Clicking on the two check boxes will ensure that the slide number and the date the slide was last altered also appear at the foot of the slide.

● Click on **Next>**.

3 THE FINISH SCREEN

● If you are happy with the content you have entered, click on **Finish** in the AutoContent Wizard's final screen. Before you do this you can move back and forth through the previous screens, making any necessary amendments.

DISPLAYING YOUR PRESENTATION ON-SCREEN

You can display your presentation in a number of different ways on your screen. Here you'll see two of the most common modes. When you first set up a new presentation, it is automatically shown in Normal view. Here the elements of your work are shown in three separate panes within the PowerPoint window. The Slide pane is on the right of the window. This is where you can view and edit the content of a single slide. The Outline pane is on the left of the window. This shows your presentation outline slide by slide. Beneath the Slide pane, you can see the Notes pane, in which you can write your own speaker's notes to accompany the slide.

The Outline pane   *The Slide pane*

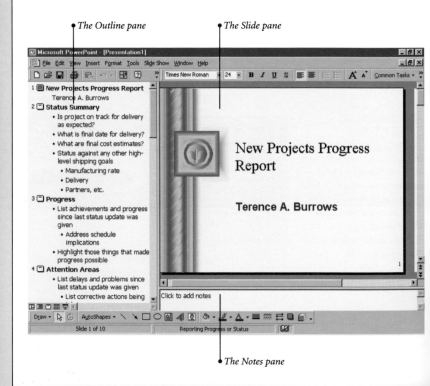

The Notes pane

RESIZING THE PANES

When you use the **Normal view** to look at your presentation, you can alter the size of any of the individual panes to suit your own needs by dragging and dropping either the horizontal or vertical borders.

● Hold the cursor over the border. You will see the pointer change from a single arrow to a double-ended arrow.

● Click on the border and drag to a new position.

● When you reach the preferred position release the mouse button.

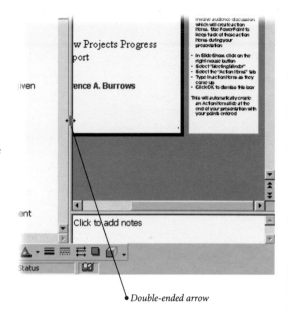

Double-ended arrow

1 LET THE SHOW BEGIN

● You can see how the presentation will look to an audience by switching to Slide Show view.

● Select **Slide Show** from the **View** menu in the Menu bar. (If you select **View Show** from the **Slide Show** menu on the Menu bar, you will achieve the same effect.)

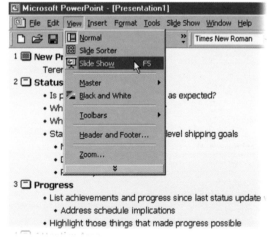

2 VIEWING THE TITLE SLIDE

● The first slide in the presentation – the Title Slide – appears, re-sized to fill the entire screen.

New Projects Progress Report

Terence A. Burrows

3 CONTINUING THE SEQUENCE

● Click on the mouse button, and the second slide in the sequence is shown on the screen. You can play through the entire sequence in this way. When you get to the final slide, click on the mouse once again to return to the previous viewing mode.

Status Summary

● **Is project on track for delivery as expected?**
● **What is final date for delivery?**
● **What are final cost estimates?**
● **Status against any other high-level shipping goals**
  – **Manufacturing rate**
  – **Delivery**
  – **Partners, etc.**

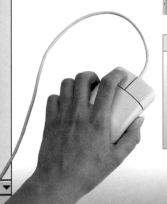

MOVING FROM SLIDE TO SLIDE

You can also work your way through the sequence using keyboard strokes. The ⏎ key advances the slide sequence in the same way as the mouse button.

The **N** (next) and **P** (previous) keys can be used to navigate back and forth between slides: the ← and → arrow keys work in the same way.

SAVING AND CLOSING

Before finishing this chapter we'll take a look at how to end a PowerPoint 2000 session. If you want to save the presentation you've been working on, you have to save it onto your hard drive. At this point you can give it a name.

1 SELECTING SAVE
● Go to **File** in the Menu bar and select **Save** from the drop-down menu.

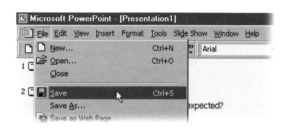

2 SELECTING WHERE TO SAVE
● The **Save As** dialog box appears. Specify the folder or drive in which you want to save your presentation by clicking on the drop-down arrow alongside the **Save in:** box and selecting from the list.

3 CHOOSING THE FILE NAME
● PowerPoint automatically suggests the same name that appears in the Title Slide. Type over it if you want to use an alternative name, and click on **Save**.

● The name you gave it will now be reflected in the dialog box's title bar.

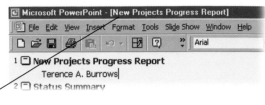

Name of presentation ●

● You can also launch the Save command from the Standard toolbar, by clicking on the **Save** tool.

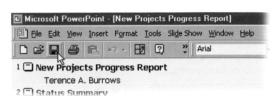

SAVE OR SAVE AS?

You may have noticed that when you pulled down the **File** menu to select the **Save** command there was another entry in the list called **Save As**. What is the difference between the two? The first time you use Save on a new presentation, PowerPoint opens the **Save As** dialog box: it is here that you specify the file name. Each subsequent time you use **Save**, no window will appear – PowerPoint simply replaces the original with the updated version.

However, if you are editing a presentation and wish to keep the original version AND the updated version, you must choose **Save As** in the **File** menu. This will invoke the **Save As** dialog box, allowing you to name the new version.

4 CLOSING YOUR PRESENTATION

● When you want to stop working on a specific presentation, you must use the **Close** command.
● Select **Close** from the **File** menu.

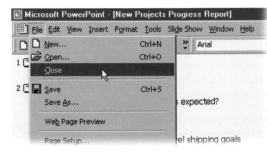

• Alternatively, you can click on the **Close** window button in the top right-hand corner of the screen.

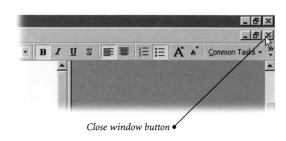

Close window button •

5 QUITTING THE PROGRAM

• When you have finished using the program you can sign off either by selecting **Exit** from the drop-down **File** menu, or by clicking on the **Close** button.

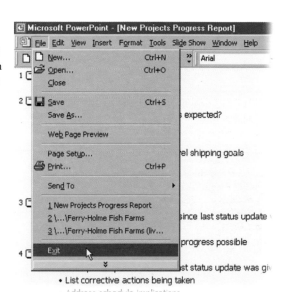

Automatic prompt
Although you should get into the habit of periodically saving your presentation as you work, if you attempt to close down before you have saved, PowerPoint 2000 will give you a handy prompt.

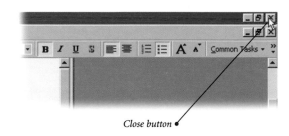

Close button •

YOUR PRESENTATIONS

An AutoContent presentation may suit your needs, but you may want to create your own slides from scratch. You can do this using either a Blank presentation or a Design Template.

A BLANK PRESENTATION

A Blank presentation is just what you would expect – it allows you to set up your presentation from scratch, with no predefined content of any kind. The way in which you set up a Blank presentation depends on whether you are just about to launch PowerPoint 2000 or you already have PowerPoint 2000 running.

1 ON LAUNCHING THE PROGRAM
● In the PowerPoint dialog box, click on the **Blank presentation** radio button and then click on **OK**.

Blank presentation radio button

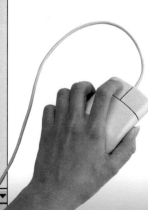

2 WHILE RUNNING POWERPOINT

● If you already have PowerPoint 2000 running, the steps are different.

● From the **PowerPoint** window, select **New** from the **File** menu.

● The **New Presentation** dialog box appears. If the options in the dialog box look different from this example, you can alter them by clicking on one of the three display buttons to the right-hand side of the dialog box.

● Click on the **General** tab and choose the **Blank Presentation** option.

● Click on **OK**.

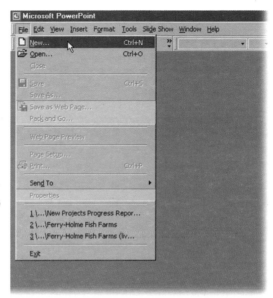

Display buttons

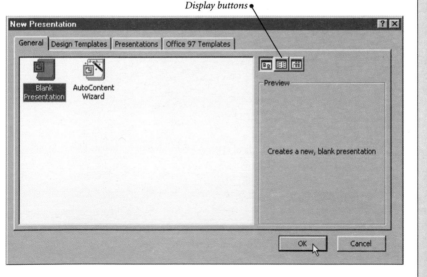

3 CHOOSING A TYPE OF SLIDE

● The **New Slide** dialog box appears. This offers you a menu of **AutoLayouts** from which to select. Each of the options provides you with a different design for a PowerPoint slide, and each contains different elements. Some, for example, contain text panels, while others contain bulleted text, charts, tables, or images. If you click on one of the icons, a description is shown on the right.

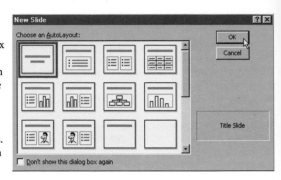

● For this example, click on the first option in the top left-hand corner of the window – the **Title Slide**.

● Click on **OK**.
● A template for the type of slide you have selected appears in **Normal view**.

Template for the title slide

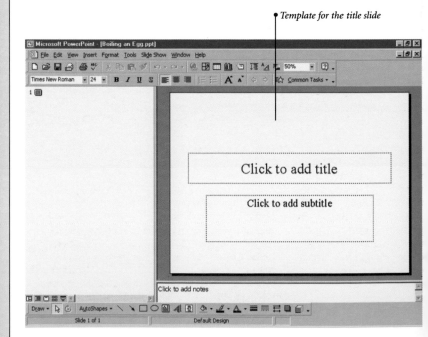

ENTERING TEXT

There are a number of different ways provided by the program that you can use to enter your text or edit what you have already inserted into PowerPoint 2000. Here you'll discover how to work on the slide using the Normal view.

1 INTRODUCING PLACEHOLDERS

● You can see from the first slide you created that there are two boxes with dotted outlines. These are known as "placeholders". They tell you that they contain a particular kind of PowerPoint object, for example text, charts, or images. When you use AutoLayouts, you will see the placeholders on the blank slide. Before you have entered any of your own text, the placeholders tell you the kind of information you need to enter. When you view the AutoLayout Title slide, you will see prompts to enter two different types of text: **title** and **subtitle**.

● To add a title, click on the placeholder marked **Click to add title**. The dotted outline changes to a shaded outline with a flashing cursor in the center.

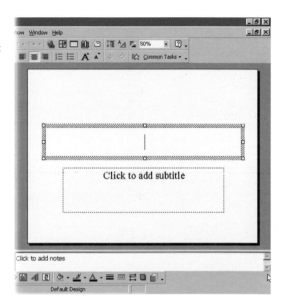

REMOVING AUTO-FITTING

There may be occasions when you have more text than will fit in the placeholder. PowerPoint 2000 automatically attempts to make the text fit in the text box. This may result in a larger text area than you anticipated. To turn off automatic fitting, choose **Options** from the **Tools** menu, click on the **Edit** tab of the **Options** dialog box, and deselect **Auto-fit text to text placeholder**.

2 TYPING IN THE TITLE

● Type in the title of the presentation that you are creating. As you do so, you will notice that the words of your title appear not only in the Slide pane where you are typing, but also in the Outline pane on the left, which can be used as a reference.

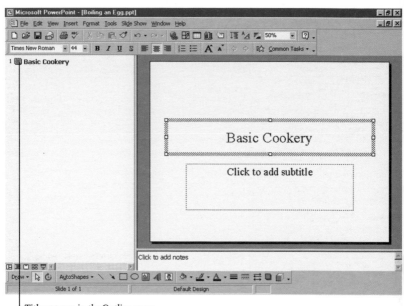

● *Title appears in the Outline pane*

3 EDITING THE TEXT

● If you want to edit your text, place the cursor at the point from which you want to edit, then drag across, highlighting the text. Release the mouse button when you reach the end point. When you type your replacement text it will automatically delete the highlighted letters.

4 ADDING A SUBTITLE

● Use the same method to add the next piece of text. Start by clicking on the placeholder labeled **Click to add subtitle**. Once again, you will notice that the new text appears in both the Slide pane and the Outline pane. This time the text of the subtitle has been indented in the Outline pane, showing that this text is at a lower level.

5 SAVING THE PRESENTATION

● Now that the first slide of the presentation has been created, the presentation can be saved.

19 Saving and Closing

ADDING A SLIDE

Any presentation is made up of a sequence of slides. We have started with the title slide, and new slides can easily be added.

The **New Slide** dialog box allows you to select from slide templates with various predefined designs and characteristics.

1 INSERTING A SECOND SLIDE

● With the Title slide set up, we can now insert a second slide into the presentation.
● Click on **New Slide** from the **Insert** menu.

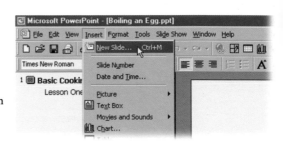

2 CHOOSING AN AUTOLAYOUT

● The **New Slide** dialog box appears. This time, choose the **Bulleted List** AutoLayout slide.
● Click on **OK**.

3 BULLET-POINTED TEXT

● Type in the text for the second slide. As you have chosen the **Bulleted List** AutoLayout, a bullet point is placed at the beginning of each new line of text.

How to Boil an Egg

- The water
- Set the burner to maximum heat
- Half-fill the pan with water
- Boil the water
- The eggs
- Put the eggs in the water
- Leave for four minutes
- Remove eggs from the water

4 ADDING A THIRD SLIDE

● Choose the AutoLayout labeled **2 Column Text**. If you look at the Outline pane, you'll see that each of the two columns of text is numbered. Enter text in the first column and press ⏎ at the end of each point. To enter text in the second column, first click in it.

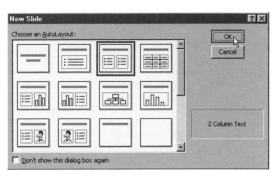

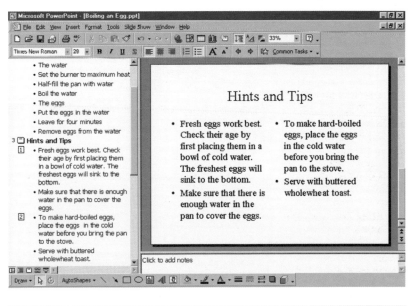

FLIPPING BETWEEN SLIDES

While you can get an overview of the presentation from the Outline pane, you can only look at the contents of one slide at a time in the Slide pane. If you click between the title and the final piece of content in the Outline pane, you will be able to view that slide in full in the Slide pane.

THE OUTLINE VIEW

You've already seen some of the different ways in which you can view a PowerPoint presentation using the Normal view. Here we'll look at another option – the Outline view. This view allows you to concentrate exclusively on the text. Although it is generally easier to edit your work within the Slide pane, the opportunity to strip away visual distractions and leave you facing the raw text in Outline view can be very useful, especially when working with complex or colorful designs.

THE VIEW TOOLBAR
You can flip between the different views by clicking on **Options** from the **View** toolbar, which you can find on the bottom left-hand corner of the dialog box.

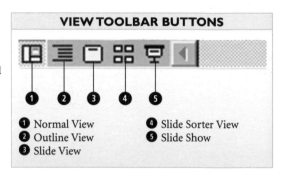

VIEW TOOLBAR BUTTONS

❶ Normal View
❷ Outline View
❸ Slide View
❹ Slide Sorter View
❺ Slide Show

SWITCHING TO THE OUTLINE VIEW
To see your presentation in the Outline view, click on the **Outline View** button.
● In Outline view, the Outline pane expands to take up most of the window. You can edit the text in the Outline pane in exactly the same way as you can in the Slide pane.

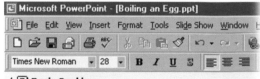

THE OUTLINING TOOLBAR

● There are a number of menu options that only take effect when you are working in the Outline view. You can access these commands via the Outlining toolbar.

● Click on **Toolbars** in the **View** menu.

● From the drop-down menu, click on **Outlining**. Alternatively, you can right-click on any toolbar and select **Outlining** from the options.

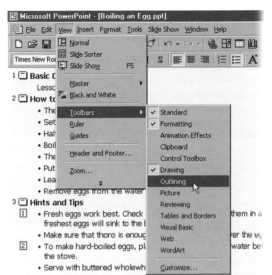

Moving the toolbar

The Outlining toolbar is displayed by default in the bottom left-hand corner of the screen. If you find it easier to use in another part of the screen, you can drag it by the title bar to anywhere in the window. The toolbar can even be dragged into the area of the toolbars below the Menu bar, where space will be made for it.

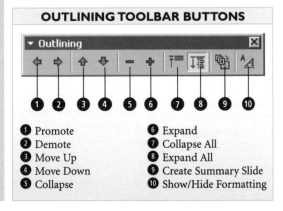

OUTLINING TOOLBAR BUTTONS

1 Promote
2 Demote
3 Move Up
4 Move Down
5 Collapse
6 Expand
7 Collapse All
8 Expand All
9 Create Summary Slide
10 Show/Hide Formatting

PROMOTING AND DEMOTING

You can structure your text on up to five different levels within each slide. This is how, for example, you can create headings and subheadings. Setting up and moving among these different levels is referred to as "promoting" and "demoting". If you look at the second slide in our presentation, you can see that the entries labeled **The water** and **The eggs** are not the same as the others on the slide. It would be more logical if they were treated as headings for the three points that follow each one. Begin by demoting the second point on the list.

1 DEMOTING TEXT

● Click anywhere within the line of text that you wish to demote. This does not include the bullet point itself, which doesn't count as regular text.
● Go to the Outlining toolbar and click on the **Demote** button.

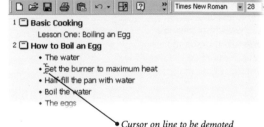

Cursor on line to be demoted

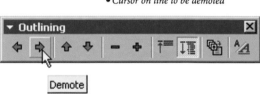

2 LINE BY LINE DEMOTION

● The line of text is now indented, showing clearly that it is a lower level than the line above, which is effectively a header.
● Repeat this process for the following two lines.

Three lines have been demoted ●

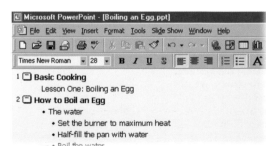

3 MULTIPLE DEMOTIONS

● Although you could demote text one line at a time, you can also perform multiple demotions on successive lines of text. Let's try this out on the three lines that follow **The eggs**.

● Place the cursor at the beginning of the first letter on line six and drag down and across to the last letter of line eight. The text on all three lines should be highlighted. Click on the **Demote** button on the Outlining toolbar.

● All three lines are now indented.

Three lines have been demoted at the same time ●

4 COLLAPSING OUTLINES

● Sometimes, especially if you have a presentation that has a large number of slides, it can be more convenient to get an overview by just looking at the titles of the slide. To do this you have to "collapse" the outline. The **Outlining** toolbar gives you two

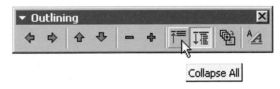

different options: you can collapse the entire presentation, or just a chosen number of slides.

● To collapse the outline of the entire presentation, click on the **Collapse All** button.

• Now only the titles are shown in the Outline pane.

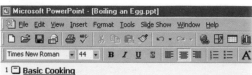

• You can reverse this action by "expanding" the outline. To do this, click on the **Expand All** button.

5 COLLAPSING A SLIDE

• To collapse just one slide, click anywhere in the title bar of the slide and then on the **Collapse** button. You can collapse a selection of slides by dragging the cursor to highlight the text before you click on the **Collapse** button.

6 CHANGING THE SEQUENCE

● You can alter the order in which the bullet points are displayed by using the **Move Up** and the **Move Down** tools.

● Highlight, or click in, the line you wish to move.

● Click on the **Move Up** button on the Outlining toolbar.

7 HIGHLIGHTED TEXT FUNCTION

● The selected point will switch places with the one immediately above. So that you can tell when a line has been moved, it remains highlighted until you next click on the mouse button.

Moving items down
To move items down within a list, you can follow the same procedures, except now use the **Move Down** button – the downward-pointing arrow.

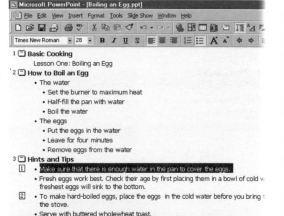

PUTTING ON THE STYLE

So far the presentations have consisted of simple black and white, text-based slides. Although there are times when this is appropriate, there are many ways to enliven your presentations.

THE DESIGN TEMPLATE

Microsoft PowerPoint 2000 comes with a wide selection of professionally designed slide templates that can be applied to your own presentations. You can use them as you create a new presentation or apply them to existing slides.

1 CREATING A NEW PRESENTATION

● Create a new presentation by selecting **New** from the **File** menu.

2 THE DESIGN TEMPLATES TAB

● The **New Presentation** dialog box opens. Click on the **Design Templates** tab.

3 VIEWING THE TEMPLATES

● Click on one of the templates to see what it looks like in the **Preview** dialog box.
● Click on the **Factory** template and click on **OK**.

4 SELECTING THE SLIDE

• The **New Slide** dialog box opens. Select the **Blank** slide option and then click on OK.

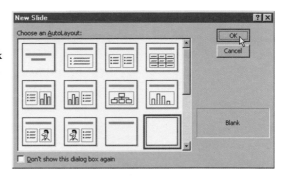

5 THE BLANK SLIDE IN NORMAL VIEW

• Once you have made your choice, you will see the blank slide displayed in Normal view with the new design in place. This design will be applied to all of the other slides you create.

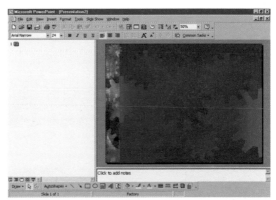

EXISTING PRESENTATIONS

Design templates need not only be applied to new presentations. You can also apply the predesigned templates to one of your existing presentations. In order to see how this works, first open the set of three slides that were created in the previous chapter.

1 OPENING AN EXISTING FILE

• Choose **Open** from the **File** menu.

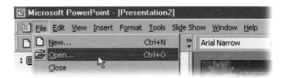

● The Open dialog box appears. Click on the presentation named **Boiling an Egg**, and then click on **Open**.

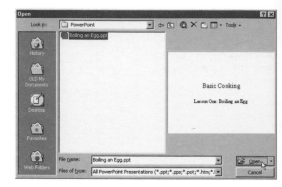

2 APPLYING A DESIGN TEMPLATE

● To select a new look for your presentation, choose **Apply Design Template** from the **Format** menu.
● The Apply Design Template dialog box appears. Select a template from the dialog box and click on **Apply**.

3 SELECTING THE DESIGN TEMPLATE

● The Apply Design Template dialog box appears. Select a template from the dialog box and click on **Apply**.

Selected design template ●

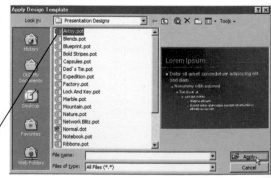

4 EFFECT OF THE DESIGN TEMPLATE

● The new template is automatically applied to your existing presentation.

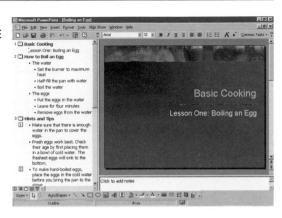

ALTERING THE TEXT

Just as you can when you use a word processor, such as Microsoft Word, PowerPoint 2000 allows you to alter the format of any of the text that appears on the slide. The easiest way to do this is by

using the Formatting toolbar ⌐. In the following example of how to alter the text, we'll change the font type and size on the Title slide of the presentation that you already have on your screen.

1 SELECTING THE TITLE

● Click on the title placeholder and position the cursor directly before the first letter. Drag the mouse across, releasing the mouse button when you pass the final character.

2 CHANGING THE FONT

● To change the font, click on the arrow alongside the **Font** list. Scroll up or down the list and choose a new and more decorative font.

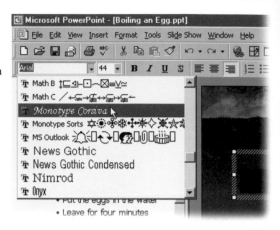

3 CHANGING THE FONT SIZE

● You can see the new typeface shown in the Slide pane. Notice, however, that the text is still highlighted. This means that any further actions you take using tools from the Formatting toolbar will still take effect on that piece of text. For example, to alter the font size, click on the arrow alongside the **Font size** list. Scroll up or down the list and choose a new size.

● Click outside the active placeholder to see the newly formatted title.

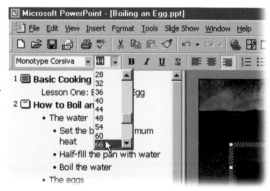

CHANGING THE BULLET POINTS

You can further alter the appearance of your presentation by changing the appearance of the bullet points. Although they are usually shown as dots or squares,

PowerPoint 2000 has a number of other options. Let's try out the various options available on the second slide of the presentation you currently have open.

1 FORMATTING THE BULLETS

● Highlight the text for the bullets you wish to change. Choose **Bullets and Numbering** from the **Format** menu.

2 CHOOSING AND RESIZING BULLETS

● The **Bullets and Numbering** dialog box opens. Click on the **Bulleted** tab to bring it to the front and select a new bullet.
● Select the size (measured as a percentage of the text) using the spin buttons.

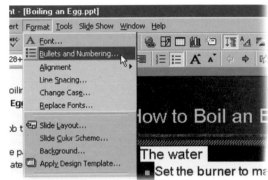

Selected bullets

Spin buttons

3 SELECTING THE BULLET COLOR
● Click on the **Color:** panel and select a color from the drop-down palette.
● Click on **OK**.

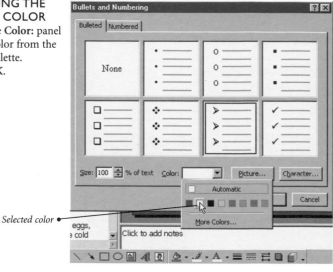

Selected color

4 VIEWING THE EFFECT
● The new-style bullet points, in the chosen color, are now shown in the slide.

PICTURES AND CHARACTERS

By clicking on either the **Picture** or **Character** buttons in the **Bullets and Numbering** dialog box, you can replace your bullet points either with alternative images, or characters from any font you have loaded on your PC.

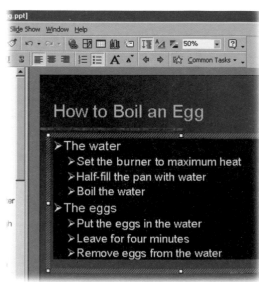

MOVING AND TRANSFORMING OBJECTS

Any of the individual elements that make up a slide are known as "objects". It is possible to alter the position of any object on a slide. In this example, one of the columns in the third slide of the presentation is to be moved.

1 SELECTING THE OBJECT

● Click on the object you wish to move. You will see that the characteristic placeholder outline appears around it.

● Position the cursor directly over the dotted outline, and the cursor changes to the directional "compass" icon.

The "compass" icon ●

2 DRAGGING THE OBJECT

● Click on the border and, with the mouse button held down, drag the object to the new location higher up on the slide. A dotted outline will show its progress.

Dotted outline ●

● Release the mouse button to drop the object in place.

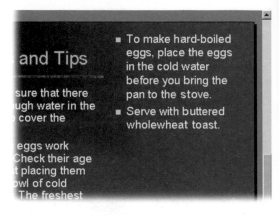

3 USING THE ARROW KEYS

● It is also possible – and easier for fine adjustment – to move objects around using the four directional arrow keys. To do this, click on the object, position the cursor directly over the border and single-click. The outline will change from a diagonal cross-shade effect to a dotted shading effect. You can then use the keyboard to reposition the object.

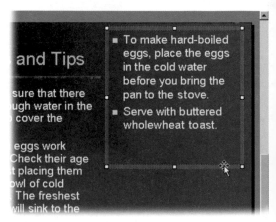

RESIZING OBJECTS

Most objects placed on a slide are given a default shape and size automatically when they are set up. These elements can also be changed at any time. You can alter the shape of a text object simply by altering the coordinates of one of the corners.

1 USING THE ARROWHEAD

● Click on the text object that you intend to resize. When you place the cursor over one of the corners, it will change its appearance to the diagonal double-arrowhead shape.

Diagonal double-arrowhead ●

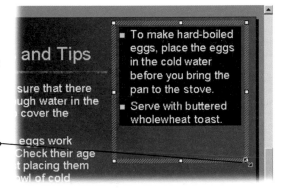

2 USING THE CROSS-HAIR

● As you drag the corner point to a new location, the cursor changes to a cross-hair and you can see the new shape of the object from the dashed outline.
● Release the mouse button when you have resized the outline as you intended.

Cross-hair cursor ●

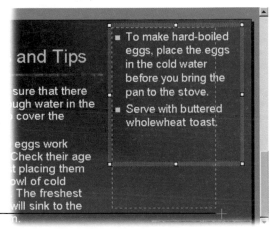

ANIMATING YOUR SLIDES

You can bring your presentations to life by using some of PowerPoint's preset animation features. To use these functions, you need to select the **Slide Sorter** view to choose a slide, and then decide on one of the preset animations.

1 SLIDE SORTER VIEW

● Click on the **Slide Sorter** button on the Views toolbar.
● Click on the slide you wish to animate.

Slide Sorter view

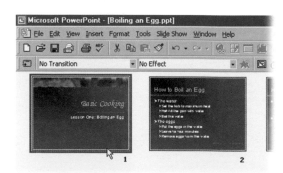

2 CHOOSING AN ANIMATION

● Select the **Preset Animation** option in the **Slide Show** menu. From the drop-down list, choose **Typewriter**.

3 RUNNING THE ANIMATION

● You will see that text on the first slide appears one character at a time and, if you have the sound on your PC switched on, you hear the sound of a typewriter. To experience the full glory of the presentation, click on the **Slide Show** button on the View toolbar.

● Notice that only the title is displayed at first. If you press the [Enter↵] key, you will see and hear the full effect of the animation.

Slide Show view

Animated text ●

THE DRAWING TOOLBAR

You don't have to rely on the designs and clip art that come as a part of the PowerPoint 2000 package to illustrate your presentations. You can create a wide range of visual effects using many of the functions found on the Drawing toolbar.

When you first launch PowerPoint 2000, the Drawing toolbar automatically appears at the foot of the dialog box. The basic drawing tools allow you to produce squares and rectangles, circles and ovals, lines and arrows. These can be styled by changing the color, adding shadows, and creating three-dimensional effects. The same working principles apply whatever drawing tool you use.

1 SELECTING THE DRAWING TOOL
● Click on the **Rectangle** tool on the Drawing toolbar.

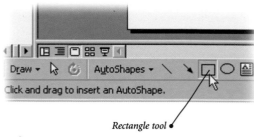

Rectangle tool ●

2 DRAWING A RECTANGLE
● The cursor changes to a cross-hair shape. Position the cursor where you want to locate one of the corners of the rectangle. Hold down the mouse button and drag the mouse toward the opposite corner of the rectangle. A dotted outline of the shape appears and changes as you move the mouse.

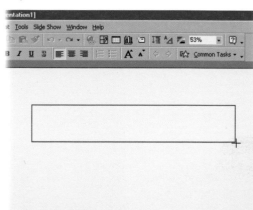

● When you release the
mouse button, the shape
will be filled automatically
with the default color
selected on the toolbar.

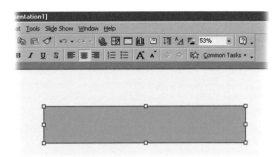

3 CHANGING THE COLOR

● To alter the color, click
on the object and then on
the arrow alongside the **Fill
Color** tool.

● The shape is now filled
with the color that you
specified. Notice that the
Fill Color tool has also
changed to reflect the
new color.

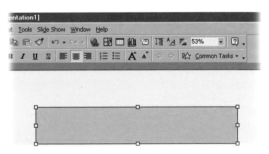

Fill Color button ●

USING WORDART

As a final word on the Drawing toolbar, we'll look at WordArt. This is an application used by Microsoft products that allows professional graphic effects to be applied to your text. This is especially useful for designing dramatic headings.

1 SELECTING WORDART

● Open a new blank slide 🗋 and click on the **Insert WordArt** button on the Drawing menu.

• Insert WordArt button

● The WordArt Gallery dialog box appears. This displays 30 different styles of WordArt for you to work with. Select one of the options and click on **OK**.

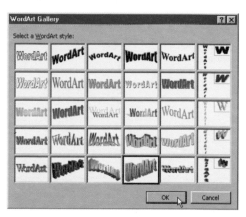

2 INSERTING AND STYLING TEXT

● The Edit WordArt Text dialog box appears. The dummy text is already highlighted, so you can type in your text straight-away. The dialog box also allows you to select the font you wish to use, its size and a limited choice of styles. When you have made your choices, click on **OK**.

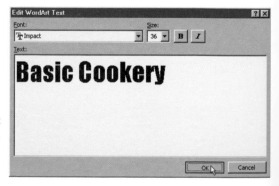

● The text is displayed on the slide.

1 CHANGING SHAPES

● Whenever a WordArt object is "active," the WordArt toolbar is displayed. This allows you to edit the object in a variety of ways.

● You can alter the appearance of your text by using the **Shapes** tool on the WordArt toolbar.

● Click on the object that you want to change and then click on the **Shapes** tool on the WordArt toolbar. Choose a shape from the pop-up menu.

● Clicking on your selection will alter the WordArt text on your slide.

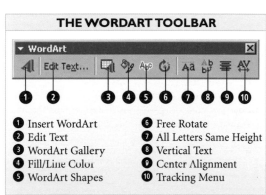

THE WORDART TOOLBAR

❶ Insert WordArt
❷ Edit Text
❸ WordArt Gallery
❹ Fill/Line Color
❺ WordArt Shapes
❻ Free Rotate
❼ All Letters Same Height
❽ Vertical Text
❾ Center Alignment
❿ Tracking Menu

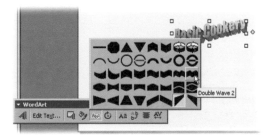

CHARTS AND TABLES

PowerPoint 2000 can be used to create almost any type of chart or graph to illustrate your presentation. In every case, the chart can be tailored very closely to meet your own needs.

CREATING A CHART

There are two straightforward ways in which you can create a chart. You can create a new slide using the **New Slide** dialog box, where you can choose an AutoLayout that already has a chart placeholder built-in. Alternatively, you can use the Insert Chart command, which is the method that we'll use in this section.

1 SELECTING CHART

● Open a new presentation and select **Chart** from the **Insert** menu.

Microsoft Graph 2000

All of the charts and graphs that appear as part of a PowerPoint presentation are created using a piece of software called Microsoft Graph 2000. This is installed and integrated with PowerPoint 2000 in such a way that it appears to be part of the program.

• You will see two things happen as PowerPoint returns you to the Normal viewing mode: a column graph has appeared in the Slide pane and a floating spreadsheet – referred to as a "Datasheet" – appears in the window.

• As you can see, the chart gives a graphical representation of the figures in the Datasheet window. PowerPoint 2000 allows you to create your own charts by replacing the sample data that is supplied in the Datasheet.

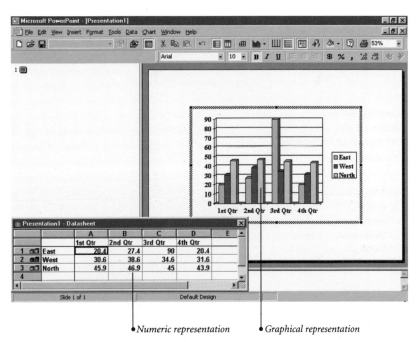

Numeric representation • *Graphical representation*

2 ADDING YOUR OWN DATA

● Each of the blocks of information on the Datasheet is referred to as a "cell". Each cell can be described in terms of its column letter and row number. For example, cell C2 currently has a value of 34.6. Replacing the information on the Datasheet is a simple matter of typing over the existing contents.

● Click on the cell you want to change. The cell is highlighted by a thick border.

● Type in the new contents as shown in our second example.

● There are several ways you can navigate around the Datasheet: you can use the directional arrows; move forward using the [Tab↹] key; back using [⇧ Shift]+[Tab↹] key; and down using the [Enter↵] key.

● You will see that each time you move to a new cell, the information you have typed in on the Datasheet is implemented on the chart.

● To see how the data you've just typed in has affected the chart, hide the Datasheet by clicking on the View Datasheet button 🗎.

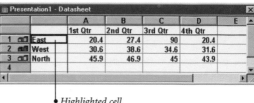

Highlighted cell

Type in the new information

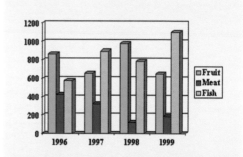

❼ View datasheet

THE GRAPH 2000 TOOLBARS

Although PowerPoint 2000 tries to make the transition to Microsoft Graph 2000 as seamless as possible, you will notice that the menu options and toolbars alter in appearance when you're using charts. This is because Graph 2000 has its own Standard and Formatting toolbars. All of the tools contained in the two toolbars can be used to alter the appearance or functionality of your chart or graph in some way. The standard toolbar is shown and labeled below.

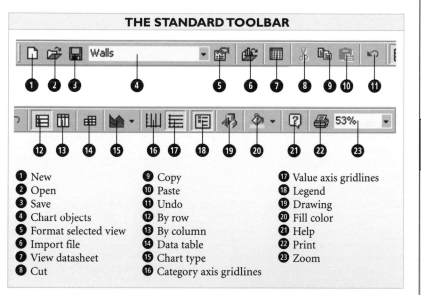

THE STANDARD TOOLBAR

1 New	**9** Copy	**17** Value axis gridlines
2 Open	**10** Paste	**18** Legend
3 Save	**11** Undo	**19** Drawing
4 Chart objects	**12** By row	**20** Fill color
5 Format selected view	**13** By column	**21** Help
6 Import file	**14** Data table	**22** Print
7 View datasheet	**15** Chart type	**23** Zoom
8 Cut	**16** Category axis gridlines	

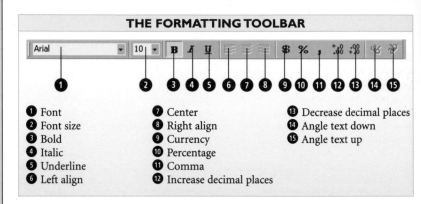

THE FORMATTING TOOLBAR

1. Font
2. Font size
3. Bold
4. Italic
5. Underline
6. Left align
7. Center
8. Right align
9. Currency
10. Percentage
11. Comma
12. Increase decimal places
13. Decrease decimal places
14. Angle text down
15. Angle text up

THE TOOLBARS IN ACTION

● Let's now see how you can customize your chart by using some of the Standard and Formatting tools. Before you do that, though, switch from Normal to Slide view ⌐. This will give you a clearer view of the chart.

● Hide the Datasheet by clicking on the **View Datasheet** tool on the Standard toolbar. This tool works like an on-off switch – click on it again and the window will reappear.

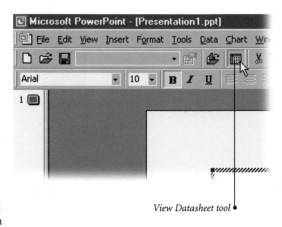

View Datasheet tool ●

FORMATTING THE DATASHEET

You can change the appearance of cells in the Datasheet by using the Formatting toolbar. After you have highlighted a cell, you can change the font type, size, and style; the positioning of text in the cell; and the number format, for example, displaying numbers as a chosen currency or as a specific number of decimal places.

❺ View toolbar buttons

• In the current Datasheet, each of the rows represents sales of fruit, meat, and fish. The columns in the Datasheet represent the years in which those sales took place. In the chart, the vertical bars are used to represent the data contained in the Datasheet rows. If you click on the **By Column** tool in the Standard toolbar, the vertical bars in the chart change to show the data contained in the Datasheet columns.

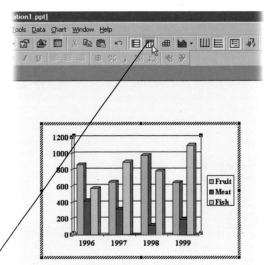

By column tool •

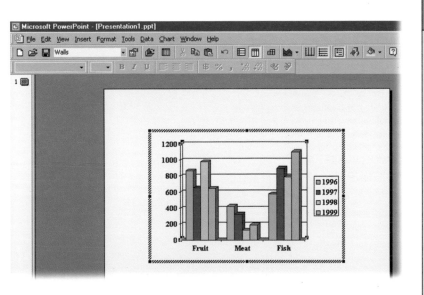

55   **⓭ By column**

DIFFERENT TYPES OF CHART

Whenever you set up a chart from scratch, Microsoft Graph 2000 defaults to the standard column graph that we've been using so far. However, there are a number of other chart styles available that can show the data in different ways.

1 CHANGING THE CHART TYPE

• It is possible to change chart types simply by using the **Chart Type** tool on the Standard toolbar. However, to see the full range of possible charts, you need to access the Chart Type dialog box.

• Select **Chart Type** from the Chart menu.

• The Chart Type dialog box appears. Click on the **Standard Types** tab at the top. The scrolling list on the left of the dialog box shows the different types of chart category that you can create. If you highlight one of the entries in the list, you will see previews of a further set of options shown on the right. Click on a chart sub-type, place the cursor over the **Press and Hold to View Sample** button, and hold down the mouse button.

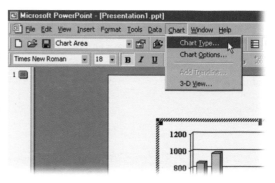

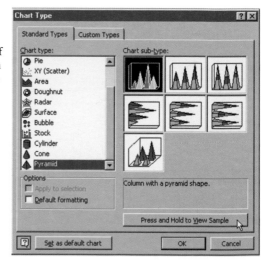

● While you are holding down the mouse button, the area containing the chart sub-types is replaced with a preview of how your original chart will look in its new form.

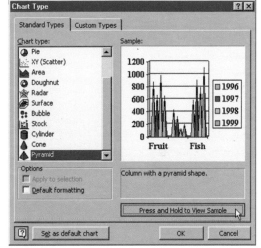

● If you want to go ahead and make the change, click on **OK**.

● Your new chart design now appears on the screen.

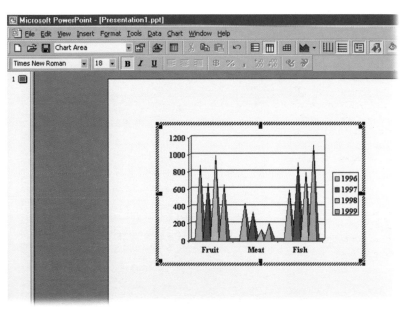

2 CHOOSING CHART OPTIONS

● A graph or chart without the correct labeling is of little value and may easily be misleading. To ensure that your chart is properly presented, use the Chart Options dialog box.

● Select **Chart Options** from the Chart menu.

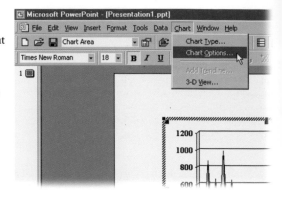

● The **Chart Options** dialog box appears. Click on the **Titles** tab at the top. Enter a title for the chart and a label for the "Value" axis. You can see a preview of the effect this has on your chart.

● Click on **OK** to see the finished chart.

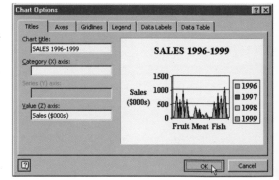

● The finished chart now fills the screen.

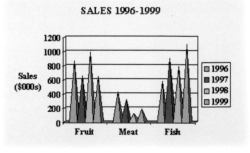

ORGANIZATION CHARTS

PowerPoint 2000 enables you to create quick, complex, and professional-looking organization charts. To do this, you must run Microsoft Organization Chart, a piece of software that is a part of the Power-Point 2000 package, and is placed on your computer during a full install. Organization Chart is a sophisticated piece of software, and only a few of its features can be shown here. If you want to investigate it further, you can work through the menus and the help screens.

1 CHOOSING THE CHART TYPE

● Open a new slide ◻ and in the **New Slide** dialog box select the AutoLayout that has an organization chart placeholder. Click on **OK**.

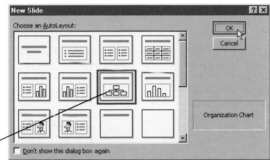

Organization chart ●

● The new slide appears. Double-click on the organization chart placeholder.

┌──┐
│28│ **Adding a slide**
└──┘

● The **Microsoft Organization Chart** program will open with a default dummy layout in place.

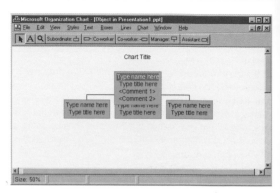

2 ADDING YOUR OWN TEXT

● Add your own details by overwriting the **Type name here** and **Type title here** lines in each box. The <**Comment 1**> and <**Comment 2**> lines can be used to hold information, such as starting date. Click outside the box to close the comment lines. To display the comment lines of the first, or any other box, click inside the box and then click on the box border.

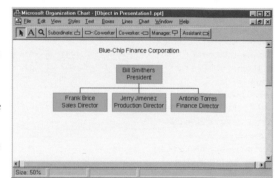

MOVING AND DELETING BOXES

One of the great benefits of the Microsoft Organization Chart is that whenever your organization changes – for example, when someone gains promotion or leaves – you don't have to create a new chart from scratch. Instead, you can adjust the existing chart by moving a box. Simply click on it, pointing to the border, and drag it over the box to which it is to be related. If you want to remove a box from the chart, simply click on it and then press the [Del] key.

3 ADDING NEW BOXES

● To add new employees to the chart, you use the buttons on the toolbar that describe the relationship you are about to create. In this instance, we'll create two subordinates to the sales director.

● Click twice on the **Subordinate** button on the toolbar. The number of times you click on that button determines the number of boxes that will automatically be created. Finally, click on the name of the individual to whom you wish to relate the two new boxes.

● Add the names and titles to the new boxes in the same way as above to complete the organization chart.

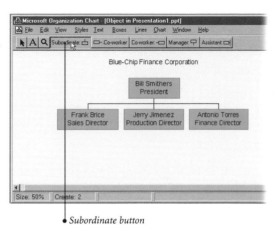

● *Subordinate button*

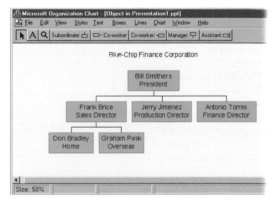

YOUR SLIDE SHOW

Finally, you'll find features including preparation, timing, and audience handouts with which PowerPoint 2000 can help you to give a more professional and convincing presentation.

PREPARING YOUR PRESENTATION

Many presentations are extremely formal, and are allocated strict time slots. Under such circumstances, your presentation needs to be carefully timed. For this to work in the most effective way, you need to work to a script. You can use PowerPoint's "Notes" feature to write a script, linking your text to each slide.

1 WRITING THE SCRIPT

● Creating your notes is easiest to do in Normal view. You simply type your text into the Notes pane, on the bottom right-hand corner of the dialog box. You'll be able to see more easily what you are doing if you drag the horizontal border with the Slide pane higher up the screen.

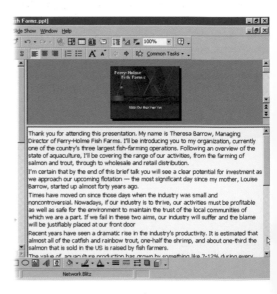

2 SELECTING THE PRINT METHOD

● To print out your script, you can either click on the **Print** tool on the Standard toolbar 🗋 or select **Print** from the **File** menu.

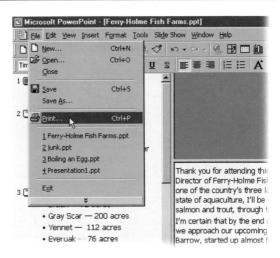

3 PRINT DIALOG BOX OPTIONS

● In the **Print** dialog box, click on the drop-down menu beneath **Print what:**. Choose **Notes Pages** from the list and click on **OK**.

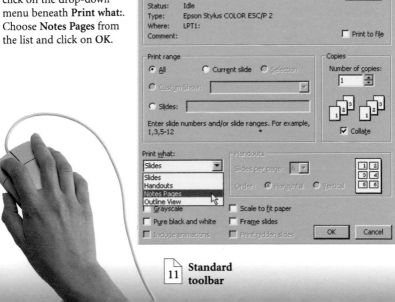

11 **Standard toolbar**

● On your print out you
will see the visual image of
the slide with your text
printed beneath.

*The slide as it will appear in
your presentation and the text
of your commentary are printed
together on your handout sheet* ●

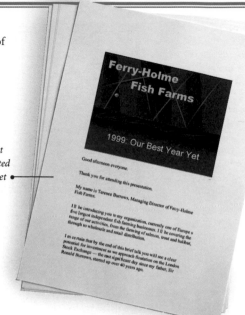

4 TIMING YOUR PRESENTATION

● Up until now, when you
have played with the **Slide
Show** view, you've had to
click through the slide
show using the mouse
button or keyboard.
PowerPoint allows you to
automate this process,
allocating precise timings
to each slide.

● Click on the **Slide Sorter**
view. Select the **Rehearse
Timings** button from the
Slide Sorter toolbar.

Rehearse Timings button ●

5 TIMING EACH SLIDE

• The first slide, the Title Slide, of your presentation appears, along with the **Rehearsal** toolbar. Begin to read your script as if you were addressing the audience. When you reach the end of your text for the first slide, click on the **Next** arrow on the Rehearsal toolbar.

THE REHEARSAL TOOLBAR

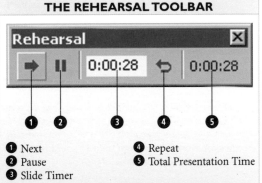

❶ Next
❷ Pause
❸ Slide Timer
❹ Repeat
❺ Total Presentation Time

• Continue in this way until you reach the final slide. You will be prompted by a box asking you if you want to record the timings that you have set up. If you do, click on **Yes**.

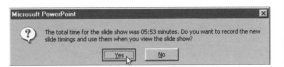

Microsoft PowerPoint

The total time for the slide show was 05:53 minutes. Do you want to record the new slide timings and use them when you view the slide show?

Yes   No

6 DISPLAYING THE SLIDE TIMINGS

● Having returned to the **Slide Sorter** view, you can see a figure below the bottom left-hand corner of each slide. This is the amount of time each slide will be displayed until automatically moving on to the next. Try the presentation out for yourself by going into **Slide Show** view.

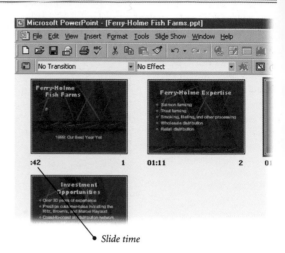

• Slide time

PRINTING AUDIENCE HANDOUTS

For your presentation to continue to have an impact once it's over, it's a good idea is to give your audience a printed copy of your presentation that they can use to

make notes and keep for their own reference. PowerPoint can produce a range of audience handouts in a number of different formats to suit your needs.

1 PRINTING THE HANDOUT

● Select **Print** from the drop-down **File** menu.

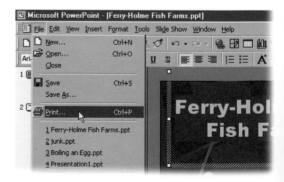

2 SELECTING PRINT OPTIONS

● In the **Print** dialog box, click on the **Print what:** drop-down arrow and select **Handouts** from the list.

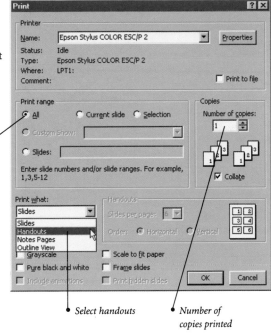

Select all slides

Select handouts

Number of copies printed

3 FORMATTING HANDOUTS

● In the **Slides per page:** area of the dialog box, click on the drop-down arrow and make your selection from the list. Audience handouts can be printed with 2, 3, 4, 6, or 9 slides on each page. Click on **OK** when you have made your choice.

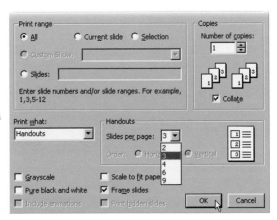

GLOSSARY

ANIMATION
Creation of moving elements within a presentation.

AUTOCONTENT WIZARD
A set of interactive instructions allowing for the selection of a series of existing presentations that can be modified for personal use.

BLANK PRESENTATION
Creating a new presentation starting with no existing design elements in place. An alternative to a pre-designed AutoContent presentation.

BULLET
Icon that appears at the start of each point in a list. PowerPoint offers a range of bullet styles.

COLLAPSING
Hiding bulleted points so that only the heading is visible.

DATASHEET
A spreadsheet-style window containing figures for use in charts and graphs. Changing the data in the sheet produces changes in the visual display.

DEMOTING
Moving bulleted items toward the bottom of the list.

DESIGN TEMPLATE
A professionally designed presentation outline that can be used as a basis for new presentations.

DRAWING TOOLBAR
Set of icons for the creation of graphic images in presentation slides.

EXPANDING
Making bulleted points visible beneath a heading. The opposite of collapsing.

FONT
The typeface in which text appears on the screen and when printed out.

FORMATTING TOOLBAR
Set of icons for altering the design of text in a presentation, such as font, type style and size, alignment and justification, and number format.

HANDOUT
Printed version of slide presentation given to the audience to accompany a presentation.

MICROSOFT GRAPH 2000
Software that can be installed with PowerPoint 2000 for the creation of charts and graphs.

NAME
Title given to a presentation before saving it on the hard drive of a PC.

NORMAL VIEW
Screen view in which text and visual elements are given equal proportions of the screen.

OBJECT
Any element of a slide, such as text, image, or sound.

ORGANIZATION CHART
A hierarchical box chart often used to illustrate the chain of command within a corporation.

OUTLINE VIEW
Screen view in which the text is the main element.

PRESENTATION
A series of linked single-screen slides viewed in sequence.

PROMOTING
Moving bulleted items toward the top of the list.

RESIZING
Dragging the edges of an object to alter its size.

SAVE
Command used to store a presentation on a PC's hard drive.

SLIDE
Single screen from a presentation.

SLIDE SHOW
Screen view in which the presentation can be viewed as a whole.

SLIDE SORTER
Screen view in which all of the slides in a presentation can be viewed in thumbnail form.

SLIDE VIEW
Screen view in which the slide design can be seen.

STANDARD TOOLBAR
A series of icons that contains shortcuts for basic functions such as opening new files or copying, cutting, and pasting objects.

WORDART
Function of the Drawing Toolbar that allows for the creation of stylized headline text in a variety of colors and shapes.